This book belongs to

David McNee

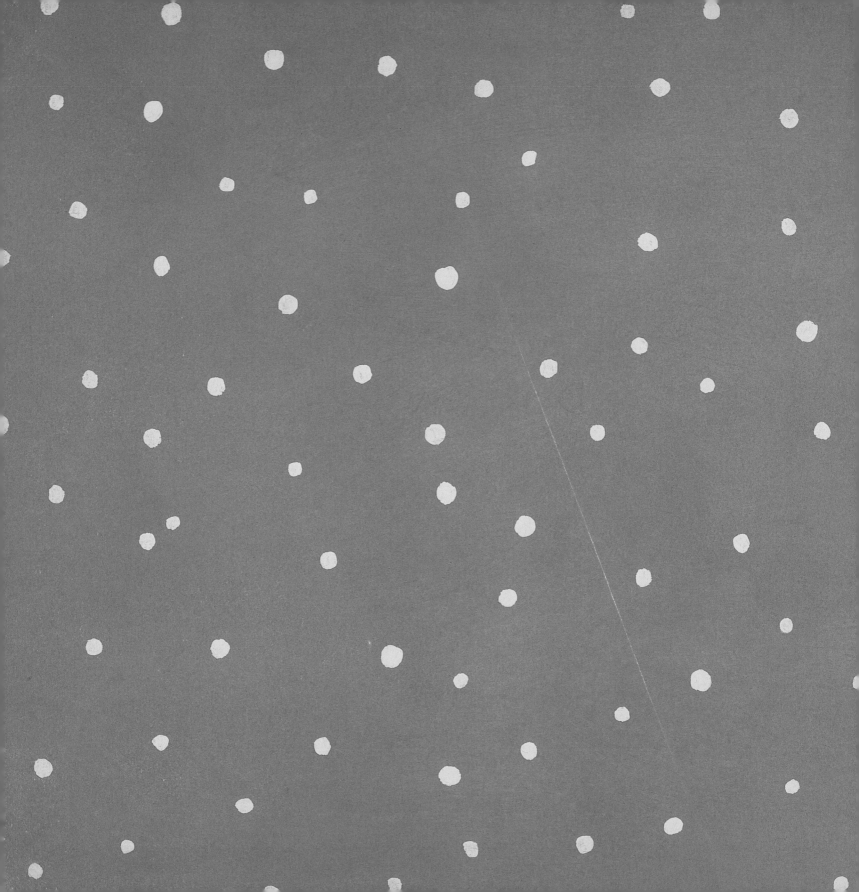

For Noah x

tiger tales

An imprint of ME Media LLC
202 Old Ridgefield Road · Wilton, CT 06897
This paperback edition published 2003
First published in the United States 2001
Originally published in Great Britain 2001 by Little Tiger Press, London
Text and Illustrations ©2001 Tim Warnes
ISBN 1-58925-376-0

Warnes, Tim.
  Can't you sleep, Dotty? / by Tim Warnes.— 1st U.S. ed.
    p. cm.
  Summary: Frustrated because she can't fall asleep in her new home
Dotty howls and wakes the neighbors, who suggest counting the stars
and other actions until, finally, they find the solution together.
  ISBN 1-58925-010-9 (hardcover)
  ISBN 1-58925-376-0 (paperback)
  [1. Bedtime--Fiction. 2. Dogs—Fiction. 3. Animals—Fiction.
4. Friendship—Fiction.] I. Title.
  PZ7.W2483 Can 2001
  [E]—dc21
                                                      2001000933

Printed in Italy
1 3 5 7 9 10 8 6 4 2

Can't you sleep, Dotty?

Tim Warnes

tiger tales

Dotty couldn't sleep.
It was her first night in
her new home.

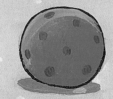

She tried sleeping
upside down.

She tried
snuggling up
to Penguin.

She even
tried lying on
the floor.

AWOOOOOOOOOOoooo

But still Dotty
couldn't sleep.

Dotty's howling woke up Pip
the Mouse. "Can't you sleep, Dotty?"
he asked. "Perhaps you should try
counting the stars like I do."

But Dotty
could only count
up to one. *That*
wasn't enough to
send her to sleep.

What could she do next?

AWOOOOOOOOOO

Susie the Bird was awake now. "Can't you sleep, Dotty?" she chirped. "I always have a little drink before I go to bed."

Dotty went to her bowl
and had a little drink.

But then she made a tiny puddle. Well *that* wouldn't help! What *could* Dotty do to get to sleep?

AWOOOOOOOOO..

Whiskers the Rabbit had woken up, too. "Can't you sleep, Dotty?" he mumbled sleepily. "I hide in my den at bedtime. That always works."

Dotty dived under her blanket so that
only her bottom was showing. But it was
very dark under there with no light at all.

Boing!

Dotty was too scared to go to sleep.

AWOOOOOOOOOOoooo

Flump!

Tommy the Tortoise
poked his head from
out of his shell.

"Can't you sleep, Dotty?" he sighed. "I like
to sleep where it's bright and sunny."

Plod
Plod

Dotty liked the idea . . .

and turned on her flashlight!

"Turn it off, Dotty!"
shouted all her friends.
"*We* can't get to sleep now!"

Poor Dotty was too tired to try
anything else. Then Tommy had
a great idea!

He helped Dotty into her bed.
What Dotty needed for the first
night in her new home was...

to snuggle among *all* her
new friends. Soon they
were all fast asleep.

Good night, Dotty.

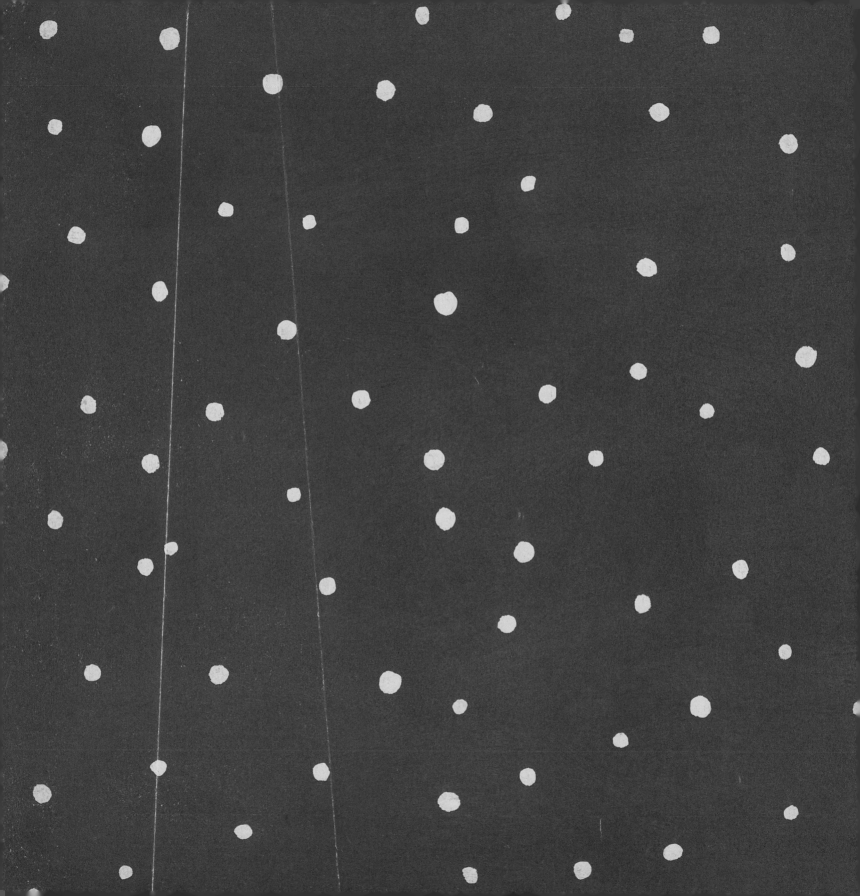

Laura's Star
by Klaus Baumgart
ISBN 1-58925-374-4

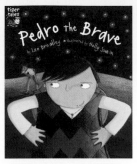

Pedro the Brave
by Leo Broadley
illustrated by Holly Swain
ISBN 1-58925-375-2

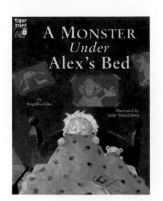

A Monster Under Alex's Bed
by Angelika Glitz
illustrated by Imke Sönnichsen
ISBN 1-58925-373-6

Explore the world of tiger tales!

More fun-filled and exciting stories await you!
Look for these titles and more at your local library or bookstore.
And have fun reading!

tiger tales

202 Old Ridgefield Road, Wilton, CT 06897

Snarlyhissopus
by Alan MacDonald
illustrated by Louise Voce
ISBN 1-58925-370-1

Commotion in the Ocean
by Giles Andreae
illustrated by David Wojtowycz
ISBN 1-58925-366-3

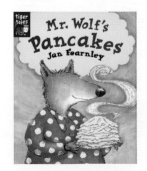

Mr. Wolf's Pancakes
by Jan Fearnley
ISBN 1-58925-354-X